East Sussex

Ben Perkins

COUNTRYSIDE BOOKS
NEWBURY BERKSHIRE

C000023544

First Published 2007
© Ben Perkins, 2007

COUNTRYSIDE BOOKS
3 Catherine Road
Newbury, Berkshire

To view our complete range of books,
please visit us at
www.countrysidebooks.co.uk

ISBN 978 1 84674 022 0

Photographs by the author
Cover picture of the South Downs near Ditchling
supplied by Derek Forss

Maps by Gelder Design & Mapping

Designed by Peter Davies, Nautilus Design
Produced through MRM Associates Ltd, Reading
Printed by Cambridge University Press

Contents

Location map   4

Introduction   5

POCKET PUB WALKS

1   Kingston, near Lewes *(5 miles)*   7

2   Chailey *(4 miles)*   12

3   Piltdown *(3 miles)*   17

4   Coleman's Hatch *(3 miles)*   22

5   Three Leg Cross *(4½ miles)*   27

6   Eridge Station *(3¾ miles)*   31

7   Blackboys *(3½ miles)*   36

8   Milton Street *(5½ miles)*   41

9   Chiddingly *(4½ miles)*   46

10   Old Heathfield *(3¾ miles)*   51

11   Cowbeech *(4½ miles)*   56

12   Boreham Street *(2½ or 4½ miles)*   61

13   Crowhurst *(3½ miles)*   66

14   Sedlescombe *(3 miles)*   71

15   Icklesham *(3¾ miles)*   76

Area map showing location of the walks

Introduction

East Sussex remains remarkably quiet and unspoilt. Once away from the built-up areas around Brighton, Eastbourne and Hastings, you are quickly into a peaceful, remote and thinly populated landscape.

Thanks to its geology and landform, the countryside has a remarkably varied character and is a magnificent area for walking. To the south of the county the chalk ridge of the South Downs, due to become part of a new National Park in the near future, reaches its abrupt and dramatic eastern end at the chalk cliffs of Beachy Head and the Seven Sisters, a designated National Heritage Coast.

To the north of the county lies the High Weald, a statutory Area of Outstanding Natural Beauty. Here is a rich landscape of ridges and valleys, where low-intensity farming has ensured that the patchwork of small fields and woodland has remained largely intact since earlier times when, in contrast to the peaceful present, the area was at the centre of the iron-smelting industry which flourished here during the 16th and 17th centuries.

Most of the walks featured in this book use paths which are clear and well signed. However, particularly in the depths of the High Weald, some of the country ways are little-used and tend to become overgrown, particularly in late summer when a stout stick might prove handy to beat down encroaching brambles.

Several of the featured pubs date back several centuries, retaining, even after modernisation, some of their original features, thus preserving the character of a traditional country ale house. I have managed to discover and include several fine old pubs which have not featured in previous books of pub walks. The walks all start and finish at the pub and most landlords have confirmed that they will allow pub patrons to use their car park while on the walk. Where the car park is small or absent, I have suggested alternative parking possibilities nearby. Even though, for good economic reasons, most landlords nowadays place a strong emphasis on catering for diners, walkers who opt for a good pint and a ploughman's are still well served.

Although I have been exploring the paths of Sussex for many years, and must have covered most of the 1,000 miles or so of public rights of way in East Sussex, there are always new discoveries to be made round every corner. It's been a great pleasure to put this book together and I wish you similar enjoyment when following in my footsteps.

Publisher's Note

We hope that you obtain considerable enjoyment from this book; great care has been taken in its preparation. However, changes of landlord and actual closures are sadly not uncommon. Likewise, although at the time of publication all routes followed public rights of way or permitted paths, diversion orders can be made and permissions withdrawn.

We cannot, of course, be held responsible for such diversion orders and any inaccuracies in the text which result from these or any other changes to the routes nor any damage which might result from walkers trespassing on private property. We are anxious though that all details covering the walks and pubs are kept up to date and would therefore welcome information from readers which would be relevant to future editions.

The simple sketch maps that accompany the walks in this book are based on notes made by the author whilst checking out the routes on the ground. However, for the benefit of a proper map, we do recommend that you purchase the relevant Ordnance Survey sheet covering your walk. The Ordnance Survey maps are widely available, especially through booksellers and local newsagents.

1 Kingston near Lewes

The Juggs

From the village of Kingston, nestling at the foot of the South Downs, this walk climbs steeply to the top of the downland escarpment, with spectacular views towards Lewes and Mount Caburn. It then drops down to explore two of the secluded dry valleys which are such a characteristic feature of the East Sussex downland. A climb up through the National Nature Reserve at Castle Hill is followed by a fine ridge walk before the descent. This is a walk to savour so allow plenty of time.

Distance - 5 miles.

OS Explorer 122 Brighton and Hove, Lewes and Burgess Hill. GR 394083.

A downland walk along good paths and tracks. One steep climb at the start.

Starting point The Juggs at Kingston, near Lewes. Park in the car park if also patronising the pub or along the lane between the pub and the Downs.

How to get there *Kingston can be accessed from the A27 at the western end of the Lewes bypass or directly from Lewes. The entrance to the pub is a few yards along The Street, a no through road signposted to the church.*

THE PUB The **Juggs**, originally a pair of tile-hung cottages dating from 1450, has been a pub since 1954. The name derives from the nickname given to the Brighton fisherwomen who used to bring their catch over the Downs from Brighton for sale in Lewes. The pub has four separate cosy bar areas, with low-beamed ceilings and a large inglenook fireplace in the main bar. Outside there is a sheltered brick patio. The Juggs is a Shepherd Neame house offering their Spitfire Premium and Kent's Best, supplemented by a seasonal ale. As well as a wide variety of good quality pub food, a snack menu includes ploughman's, jacket potatoes, soup and 'doorstep' sandwiches. Children and dogs are equally welcome.

Opening times: 11 am to 11 pm on Monday to Saturday and 12 noon to 10.30 pm on Sunday. Food is served Monday to Saturday from 12 noon to 2.30 pm and 6 pm to 9 pm and on Sunday from 12 noon to 8 pm. ☎ *01273 483274*

1 Start the walk along **The Street**, passing the old flint-walled village pound on the left and the church on the right. Where the lane ends, go ahead along a rough track. Soon after passing through a swing gate, go left over a stile and follow a clear path which rises steadily through woodland and then more steeply over grass downland before skirting along the edge of a deep combe. Just before reaching the summit of the escarpment bear right along a track.

2 Cross the **South Downs Way**, go through a gate to the left of a cattle grid and drop downhill on a clear chalk and flint track which, beyond a barn, continues along the grassy floor of

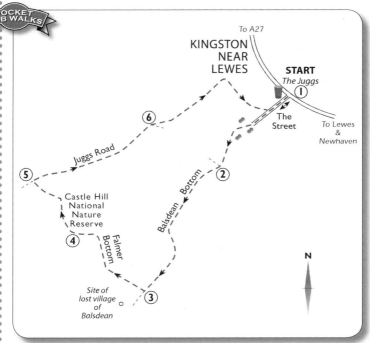

Castle Hill National Nature Reserve.

Balsdean Bottom. Where you have a choice of two gates in a crossing fence, go through the right-hand bridlegate, forward to a similar gate and on along the valley floor.

3 A few yards short of a group of barns and sheds, partly in ruins, turn right. This remote valley is the site of the 'lost' village of **Balsdean**, where a small 12th-century chapel stood until the Second World War. Your path now follows the right-hand side of another dry downland valley, **Falmer Bottom**.

4 After about half a mile, you will come to gate where there is a notice indicating that you are entering **Castle Hill National Nature Reserve**, a rare example of untouched chalk downland, parts of which have not been ploughed for hundreds of years. It supports a wide variety of plants and insects, including a colony of rare wartbiter crickets. Through the gate, ignoring a path to the left, bear right along a track which, at first, contours along the lower slopes of a side valley within the nature reserve, then gains height as it passes between areas of scrub before emerging

from the top end of the valley to join a crossing track at the edge of the reserve. A dispenser attached to a notice offers a useful leaflet with information about the area.

5 Turn right along this track. Beyond a gate you have a choice of two roughly parallel routes ahead. Either will do, but the unfenced left-hand path is probably the better of the two and is also the official right of way. It follows a ridge, keeping fairly close to the steep slope dropping down on your left and offers good views across the valley. This path is indicated on the map as part of the **South Downs Way** and also as **Juggs Road**.

6 Beyond a new bridlegate, the **South Downs Way** bears away to the right but you should go ahead, keeping close to a left-hand fence with **Lewes** directly ahead, soon entering a sunken track. The village of **Kingston** comes into view, tucked in at the foot of the Downs. On the other side of the valley, behind Lewes, you get a good view of an outlying area of downland rising to **Mount Caburn**. At the edge of the village turn right along a signed bridleway which starts between wooden posts. The path becomes a gravelled track and then **Church Lane**. Shortly go half left across a recreation ground. From the far corner a path leads out through **Kingston churchyard** to join a lane. Turn left back to the start.

Places of interest nearby

The ancient county town of **Lewes**, only two miles from Kingston, has much to offer. You can climb to the top of the 12th-century **Lewes Castle**, with commanding views across the town, (☎ 01273 486290), or visit **Anne of Cleves' House,** a 16th-century, timber-framed building given to Henry VIII's fourth wife. It is open daily during the summer months and from Tuesday to Saturday in winter. ☎ 01273 474610.

2 Chailey

The Five Bells

This easy walk, without significant hills, offers an opportunity to explore Markstakes Common, a delightful area of ancient woodland in the Low Weald to the north of Lewes. It uses sections of two historic green lanes, once roads but now quiet leafy tracks, though some care is needed when navigating a route across the common where it is easy to go astray along one of the many alternative paths which criss-cross the area.

THE PUB

The **Five Bells** was once a coaching inn and may have derived its name from the coachman's habit of ringing a bell as each milestone was reached. The inn coincided with the sounding of the fifth bell out of Lewes. It is a spacious pub, the oldest part of the building dating from the 15th century. The main bar has a brick floor and a log fire, and there is a newer dining area housed in an extension at the rear. It is now an Enterprise Inn, specialising in high quality, home-cooked food using locally-produced ingredients. There is no snack menu as such though you can choose from 'light lunch' dishes on the main menu and ciabattas, with interesting fillings such as crayfish and prawns in spiced mayonnaise, are on offer at lunchtime.

Opening times: 12 noon to 3 pm and 6 pm to 11 pm except Sunday and Monday evening. Food is served from 12 noon to 2.30 pm and 6.30 pm to 9.30 pm.
☎ *01825 722259*

Distance - 4 miles.

OS Explorer 122 Brighton and Hove, Lewes and Burgess Hill. GR 394191.

A level walk which may be muddy in places after rain.

Starting point The Five Bells pub at Chailey. Park in the pub car park with permission, or along Markstakes Lane (GR 398184), joining the walk at point 2.

How to get there *The Five Bells is on the west side of the A275 Lewes-to-East Grinstead road, about 5 miles north of Lewes.*

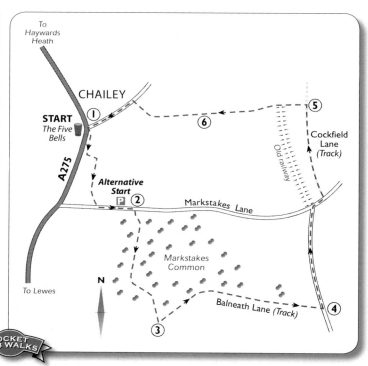

1. From the pub, turn right and, after a few yards, go left over a stile and follow a path which runs parallel to the main road, behind the roadside hedge and within a grove of planted trees. After about 150 yards, go left through a gap in these trees to a stile and then ahead across a field. On the other side of the field go through a gap in the hedge next to a large tree and turn right to follow the edge of the next field and out to join **Markstakes Lane**. Turn left.

2. After about 250 yards, go right through a double gate in a flint wall and ahead on a clear path into the woodland of **Markstakes**

Common, soon crossing a stream. Shortly, fork left along a path which crosses a more open area of the common. About five yards short of a waypost, bear right. Ignore the next left fork and, at a waypost where there is a rustic seat nearby, turn left on a clear path through thicker woodland. Shortly, at another waymarker, fork right, and descend to cross a plank bridge. Where the path divides yet again, fork left. At the next two wayposts keep straight ahead following the direction of yellow arrows.

3 At a junction with a wider path, turn left and follow this heavily-used route eastwards. At a meeting of a number of paths, turn squarely right with the main track. Approaching the edge of the wooded area, turn left to follow a wide track between low banks, running parallel to the edge of the wood. This is **Balneath Lane**, an old road, which you can now follow for two thirds of a mile to a road.

Markstakes Common.

4 Turn left and, after about half a mile, turn right at a road junction, signposted to **Newick**. After 150 yards, go left along another substantial tree-lined track. This is **Cockfield Lane**, another old highway. To the left of the path, hidden in the trees, you can make out a raised embankment which once carried the railway line between **Lewes** and **Uckfield**.

5 After another half a mile, turn left over a stile from which a trodden path heads out across a field to a second stile. Cross a bridge over the old railway, skirt to the right of an area of scrub and bear slightly left across an area of rough pasture where there is a faint path which drops gently down and feeds into a track which skirts to the left of the end of a long, thin pond.

6 Once out into the next field, a useful fingerpost points the direction across another large field, where once again a path is discernible. Pass another fingerpost and continue to a stile where a pair of silver birch trees, planted in 1984, mark the line of the **Greenwich Meridian**. Go forward to join and follow the drive from a house. After 60 yards along this drive, bear half right across grass to join a lane. Turn left and follow the lane back to the A275, opposite the pub.

Places of interest nearby

Sheffield Park Garden is 4 miles to the north of Chailey along the A275. This fine, landscaped garden was first laid out by 'Capability' Brown in the 18th century. It is notable for spectacular displays of azaleas and rhododendrons in the spring and for its leaf colours in autumn. It is a National Trust property open from 10.30 am to 6 pm except Mondays (more restricted opening times during the winter months).
☎ *01825 790231*

3 Piltdown

The Piltdown Man

The **modest community of Piltdown** would barely register on the map were it not for the remarkable story of the Piltdown Skull, discovered in a local gravel pit in 1912. It was, at first, thought to be the remains of a 150,000-year-old man, but following tests carried out in 1953, was proved to be a fake. Passing close to the site of the 'discovery' near Barkham Manor, this walk follows field paths in the valley of the River Ouse.

THE PUB

The **Piltdown Man** has been a pub for 100 years. Previously the Lamb Inn, it acquired its present name following the discovery of the skull and jawbone of a 'missing link' apeman, and has retained the name even though the jaw turned out to be a modern forgery. It is a freehouse which has recently undergone extensive refurbishment. It is now a family-orientated establishment, with an elaborate adventure playground and pet farm, as well as an old-fashioned sweet shop. Inside there are two bars and a separate dining area. The food menu is an extensive one, all home-cooked and includes popular main dishes, as well as a choice of lighter meals, including ciabatta sandwiches or baguettes with a variety of interesting fillings. The beer on offer is the local Harveys Bitter and a regularly-changing guest ale.

Opening times: 11 am to 11 pm on Monday to Saturday and 12 noon to 11 pm on Sunday. Food is served until 10 pm daily.
☎ *01825 723563*

1 From the pub, turn left along the near-side pavement beside the A272. After 150 yards, turn left along the gravel drive to a house called **Stonelands** which soon narrows to a path which may be

Distance - 3 miles.

OS Explorer 135 Ashdown Forest. GR 440222.

A walk beside an old vineyard and across low-lying water meadows, liable to flooding in winter. One muddy path beyond Sharp's Bridge.

Starting point The Piltdown Man at Piltdown. Patrons may park in the pub car park while on the walk. Alternative parking next to Piltdown Pond at GR 443222.

How to get there *Piltdown is on the A272, about 3 miles west of Uckfield.*

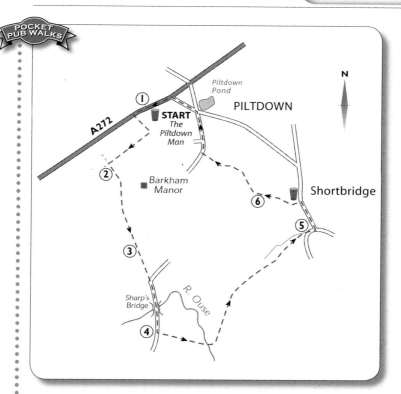

overgrown. After a little over 100 yards, go right over a stile and forward along the right edge of a field, divided by the remains of hedges, once the shelter belts of a former vineyard.

2 Cross a drive, go over a footbridge and, ignoring a stile on the right, go left along a left field edge with a row of tall trees on your left, another shelter belt. Skirt to the right of the elaborately landscaped garden and ornamental pond of **Barkham Manor.** Follow the field edge left, then right until you can go left through a wide gap.

Piltdown Pond.

3 A few yards beyond this gap, veer half left across the middle of a cultivated field where there should be a faint path through any growing crop. Once over a low rise, aim just to the left of a cottage where, in the field corner you can join a lane over a stile. Bear right along the lane to cross **Sharp's Bridge** over the **River Ouse**. A raised walkway beside the road and a water depth indicator are reminders that this is an area at risk of winter flooding.

4 After another 150 yards, just after passing the entrance to **Sharpsbridge Farm**, turn left over a stile to follow a left field edge. Where the hedge turns away to your left, go straight ahead across a field to a squeeze stile in the next hedge. Go ahead for a few yards to a bridge over the **River Ouse**. Once over this bridge, go half left across a low-lying water meadow. From the other side of this field a clear path continues with a stream nearby on your left. Where you have a choice of waymarked paths keep left, still close to the stream. The path can be muddy and overgrown in places but boardwalks have been provided to get you across the worst bits. Follow this path out to a lane.

5 Turn left and immediately left again along **Shortbridge Road**. Just short of the **Peacock Inn**, turn left along a tarmac drive. After less than 100 yards, side-step to the left over a sleeper bridge and turn right to follow a right field edge. From this path you get a good view southwards to the ridge of the **Downs** to the west of **Lewes**, with the tree clump on **Blackcap** a distinctive feature.

6 After about 250 yards, go right through a gap in the hedge and follow a woodland path which soon comes out onto **Piltdown Golf Course.** Follow the left edge of the play area, keeping a lookout for a post on the left directing you back into the wood. Once inside the wood, turn right, keeping close to the wood edge before re-emerging onto the golf course. Once again follow the edge of a play area. Ignoring a waymarked path pointing half right, go ahead between the two eighth tees and immediately turn left for a few yards to join a track. Turn right and follow this track out to a road. Turn right and, at a road junction, go ahead. At a second road junction next to **Piltdown Pond**, turn left. Ignore a right fork and, after 150 yards, at the A272, turn left back to the pub.

Places of interest nearby

A few miles to the north-west of Piltdown via the A272 and A275 is the southern terminus of the restored **Bluebell Railway**, where you can enjoy a steam-hauled train ride through the Sussex countryside between Sheffield Park and Horsted Keynes. ☎ *01825 720825.*

The Hatch Inn

As the name implies, the scattered settlement of Coleman's Hatch, first established in the 14th century, stands at one of the 'hatches' or gateways into Ashdown Forest. Although the open forest is within easy reach, our walk turns north to explore an intimate landscape of small fields divided by hedgerows, rich in mature trees on the lower slopes of the valley of the River Medway, close to its source. The walk is an easy one, without significant hills, using well established paths and quiet lanes.

THE PUB

The **Hatch Inn** started life as a row of mill-workers' cottages in 1430. It became an inn during the 18th century and, in its early days, was reputed to be the haunt of rum smugglers. It remains a compact and cosy pub, with a low-ceilinged bar and a snug dining area at the rear, as well as a large garden. It is a

Distance - 3 miles.

OS Explorer 135 Ashdown Forest. GR 452333.

A gently undulating walk.

Starting point The Hatch Inn at Coleman's Hatch. The pub does not have a car park, but you should find room to park beside Kidd's Hill or near the pub.

How to get there From the B2110 Forest Row-to-Hartfield road about 2 miles east of Forest Row, turn south along Shepherd's Gate, opposite Coleman's Hatch church. At the next junction go left and immediately left again into Kidd's Hill within a few yards of the pub.

free house serving Harveys Sussex Bitter and traditional ale from Larkins Brewery of Chiddingstone in Kent, as well as two rotating guest beers. The extensive menu, changed daily, comprises a long list of substantial main dishes, as well as more traditional walkers' fare. The ploughman's comes with a choice of unusual British cheeses such as Cornish Yarg or Smoked Applewood, and the sandwiches have original fillings such as crayfish tail or brie and apple. Children and dogs are welcome.

Opening times: 11.30 am to 2.30 pm and 5.30 pm to 11 pm on Monday to Saturday and from 12 noon to 10.30 pm on Sunday. Food is served from 12 noon to 2 pm and 7 pm to 9 pm except on Monday evening.
☎ *01342 822363*

1 From the pub, turn right down **Kidd's Hill**. At the bottom of the hill, turn left through a kissing-gate and head squarely along

the valley, passing several fine mature oak trees. Go through a second gate and follow the right edge of two fields. Join **Harts Lane** down stone steps and turn right.

2 At a road junction turn left along **Marsh Green Lane**. After about 400 yards, turn sharply back to the left along a gravel drive, passing to the right of the gateway to **Old School House**. The drive narrows to a path within a strip of woodland and crosses a footbridge. A well-trodden path takes you across an area of rough pasture, over a wide sleeper bridge and up to the top corner of this rough grassy area.

3 Once over a stile, where you have a choice of two signed paths, fork left along the left edge of an area of planted trees, through a gate and forward, passing to the right of a tennis court. Go over

The pond passed at point 5 of the walk.

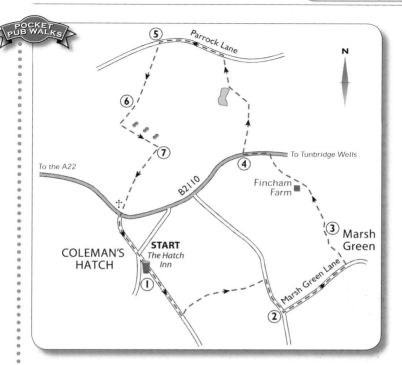

POCKET PUB WALKS

a stile, ahead to a second stile and half left across the corner of a paddock to find a third stile hidden behind an oak tree. Turn right to follow the drive from **Fincham Farm** out to the **B2110** where you turn left.

4 After 150 yards, just past the entrance to **The Pond Cottage**, turn right along a wide fenced path. After skirting to the left of a cottage, resume your previous direction across a field to go through a gateway and across the next field to a second gate. Veer half left across the field beyond to a third gate in the corner from which a tree-lined path continues to join **Parrock Lane**. Turn left.

5 Soon after passing a white, weather-boarded cottage on the left called **Parrock Brook**, and immediately after the road crosses a tiny stream, turn left along a path which winds through an area of trees and scrub, passing to the right of a pond with a stream to the left. After about 200 yards, go through a gate and forward along a left field edge to a second gate. Now bear half right up across the middle of a horse paddock.

6 In the far top corner of the field, go over a stile and bear right to follow a right-hand post and rail fence along the right edge of another large paddock. Go over a stile a few yards to the left of the next field corner and follow a path through a belt of woodland. On the far side of the wood, the path officially goes left round two sides of a field, but there is a trodden path half left across the middle of the field used by many walkers.

7 Either way, from the far corner of this area a path passes through woodland to a gate. Here, where you have a choice of signed paths, go half right across a field to a stile in the far corner from which a clear woodland path continues out to the **B2110** next to **Coleman's Hatch church**. Cross the road and follow **Shepherd's Gate**, opposite. At a road junction, turn right and immediately left, back to the pub, a few yards away.

Places of interest nearby

The **Ashdown Forest Centre**, about 1½ miles along the road from Coleman's Hatch to Wych Cross, is a good starting point for exploring Ashdown Forest. It offers maps and leaflets, as well as a small exhibition. Opening times are from 11 am to 5 pm at weekends and from 2 pm to 5 pm on weekdays during the summer months. Pooh Sticks Bridge, one of the most famous forest sites, is within easy walking distance of the Hatch Inn at GR 470339.

5 **Three Leg Cross**

The Bull

The main focus of this walk is Bewl Water, the largest area of open inland water in south-east England. Covering 770 acres and containing almost 7,000 million gallons of water when full, it was constructed between 1972 and 1975. The 15-mile shoreline is encircled by a 13-mile perimeter path which we will be sampling on this walk, starting and finishing at the small settlement of Three Leg Cross to the south of the reservoir. Bewl Water provides an important wildfowl habitat and the water authority have set aside a designated 127-acre site as a nature reserve, though, sadly, the public are excluded from this protected area.

THE PUB The **Bull** is housed in one of the oldest buildings in the area, dating from the 14th century, though it has been a pub for a mere 150 years or so. It enjoys a beautiful setting, surrounded by a spacious 4-acre garden, with a small pond and aviary, as

Distance - 4½ miles.

OS Explorer 136 High Weald. GR 686311.

An easy, level walk, almost entirely along good paths and quiet lanes.

Starting point The Bull Inn at Three Leg Cross, near Ticehurst. Patrons may park in the pub car park with prior permission. Limited roadside parking near the pub.

How to get there *The village of Ticehurst is on the B2099 road linking Wadhurst with the A21 at Flimwell. Three Leg Cross is signposted northwards along a lane from the B2099, at the western end of the village.*

well as a play area for children. Inside, the bar is divided into several cosy areas, with low-beamed ceilings and tiled floors, and a modern dining room at one end. It is a free house serving the local Harveys Sussex Bitter, plus three guest beers. The food menu is a varied one, comprising pub favourites like cottage pie and a choice of meat or vegetable lasagnes at lunchtime, as well as snacks such as ploughman's, filled baguettes and jacket potatoes. In the evening the menu is supplemented by more classy 'specials' such as salmon and crayfish linguini. Children and dogs are welcome and the pub also offers bed and breakfast.

Opening times: 11 am to 11 pm on Monday to Saturday and 12 noon to 10.30 pm on Sunday. Food is served in the restaurant from 12 noon to 2.30 pm and 6.30 pm to 9 pm on Monday to Friday except Monday evening and from 12 noon to 3 pm on Sunday (no food Sunday evening).
☎ *01580 200586*

1 From the pub, start the walk along **Borders Lane** which passes to the left of the pub and heads generally westwards between high hedges. At a road junction turn right and, at a second junction, go right again, now on a signed no through road.

2 Beyond two gates in quick succession, the road feeds into the **Round Bewl Water Path**. This well-surfaced path is open to equestrians and cyclists, as well as walkers, so some care is needed to avoid clashes, though pedestrians do, in theory, have priority of access at pinch-points. The path meanders round an inlet and then heads down beside a second minor creek.

3 Just short of a gate, where the main **Round Bewl Water Path** is

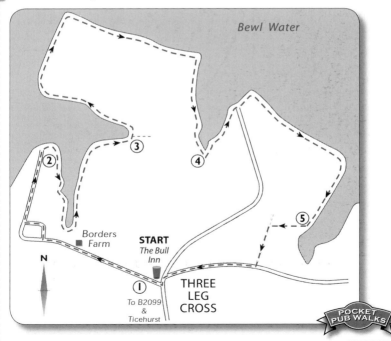

signed ahead, you should turn left along a narrower path which is a permissive pedestrian route, not marked on the Explorer Map. It is overgrown at first but then comes out into the open to round a headland with an expanding view along **Bewl Water** to the reservoir dam and the water draw-off and overflow towers, and across to the **Bewl Water Visitor Centre**. As you round another corner and, after passing through a small wooded area, a new view unfolds along **Bewl Straight** towards the far eastern end of the reservoir.

4 Beyond a stile beside a gate, the main **Bewl Water** path rejoins from the right and you can go ahead along it, now shaded by trees. The path joins the end of a road which once crossed the valley but now disappears into the water. Turn right for a few yards, then just past a barrier, turn left, continuing along the **Round Bewl Water Path**. Follow this delightful path as, partly out in the open, partly shaded by trees, it rounds another headland and continues along the side of an inlet.

5 After another half a mile or so, turn right along a signed path which passes between tree-lined banks and may be muddy as it doubles as a small stream at times. At a path junction, turn left, still between banks. Follow this path out to a lane where you should turn right for about a quarter of a mile back to **Three Leg Cross**. At a road junction turn left for a few yards back to the start.

Places of interest nearby

Pashley Manor Gardens are on the B2099 about a mile south-east of Ticehurst. Described on its website as a 'quintessential English garden'. The house is not open to the public but the gardens are open April to September from 11 am to 5 pm on Wednesday, Thursday, Saturday and Bank Holiday Mondays. ☎ *01580 200888*.

6 **Eridge Station**

The Huntsman

Situated in the centre of the High Weald to the south of Tunbridge Wells, Eridge Station is an excellent starting point for several walks exploring this rich landscape of sandstone ridges and quiet valleys. Starting from the station, once a busy junction but now a halt on the single remaining railway linking Uckfield with Oxted, the walk heads southwards, climbing steadily to Boarshead before dropping down to cross a secluded and beautiful valley.

THE PUB | The **Huntsman**, extensively refurbished in 2006 and now bypassed by the busy A26, is tucked away in a loop of the old redundant road next to Eridge railway station. The patio at the front of the pub and the decked area at the rear are protected by large awnings and an outside bar operates during summer weekends. The well-kept beer on offer includes King and Barnes Sussex, Badger's First Gold or, for a change, 'Stinger' Nettle Beer. You can also choose from an award-winning wine list. The interesting menu, changed daily, concentrates on locally-sourced produce, including game. Sandwiches are available or, if you are feeling particularly hungry, you might like to try the Huntsman's Platter, a rather grand ploughman's with turkey, ham and pâté pie as well as cheese. Children and dogs are welcome.

Opening times: 11.30 am to 2.30 pm and 5.30 pm to 11 pm on Tuesday to Saturday and 12 noon to 4 pm and 7 pm to 11 pm on Sunday. Food is served from 12 noon to 2 pm and from 7 pm to 9 pm. The pub is closed on Mondays.
☎ *01892 864258*

Distance - 3¾ miles.

OS Explorer 135 Ashdown Forest. GR 543346.

A fairly hilly walk along field paths, mostly well established except for one path across an arable field.

Starting point The Huntsman Inn at Eridge Station. Roadside parking is plentiful at weekends but at a premium during the week when rail commuters occupy every available space but leave ample room in the station car park (fee payable).

How to get there *Eridge Station is signposted from the A26 Crowborough-to-Tunbridge Wells road about three miles north of Crowborough. The pub is a few yards past the station entrance.*

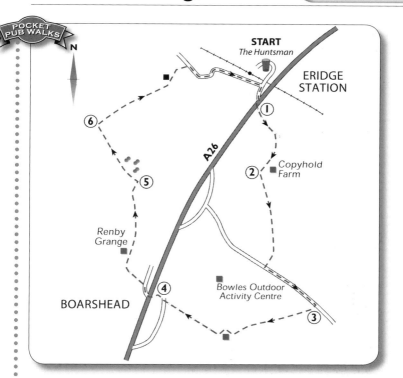

START
The Huntsman

ERIDGE STATION

①

② *Copyhold Farm*

Renby Grange

⑤

⑥

③

④

Bowles Outdoor Activity Centre

BOARSHEAD

N

A26

1. Return to the main A26 road, turn right for a few yards and then go left along a tarmac drive marked with a stone plinth as a public footpath. After about 250 yards, just past a pond on the right, (not marked on the Explorer map), fork right to a gate and climb beside a fence on your right. At the field corner go through a gate and forward for a few yards before bearing right along the gravel drive from a large weather-boarded and tile hung house (**Copyhold Farm**).

2. After about 100 yards, fork left on a path indicated by a fingerpost which takes a fairly level route across a large cultivated field. Pass

to the right of a line of trees and a ditch protruding into the field from the left and continue across the field to join a lane. Turn left, soon passing, on your right, the entrance to **Bowles Outdoor Activity Centre**.

3 After 350 yards, turn right up a slope to a gate, set back from the lane, and go forward along the right edge of a field. Through a gap in the hedge on your right you get a good view of the dramatic sandstone outcrop in the **Bowles Centre**, used for climbing practice. Follow a headland track which, after a quarter of a mile, goes through a gap before bearing left and then right to head for the buildings at **Rocks Farm** with the dry ski slope at the **Bowles Centre** in view. Approaching the farm, follow the signed path as it skirts to the right of the buildings. Join and follow the access drive from the farm out to a road at the end of a cul-de-sac, once the main A26.

On the path beyond Renby Grange.

4 Turn right to follow a path which ramps down to cross the present A26 and then ramps up the other side. On reaching the end of another cul-de-sac road, turn left along a tree-lined, patchily concreted access drive which drops down between banks. Ignoring a left fork, pass to the right of **Little Renby** and **Renby Grange**. After another 100 yards, side-step to the left over a stile and resume your previous direction, after a few yards entering a fine, old, tree-lined hollow way.

5 After about 300 yards, where the path begins to open out, turn left at a fingerpost and drop downhill along a concrete track between banks. At the bottom of the hill go forward for about 40 yards before going right over a stile. Now climb diagonally up across the middle of a field. In the field corner go ahead, passing a tree-shrouded pit on your right before heading out across a field.

6 On the other side of this field, turn right with a hedge on your left. In the field corner go through a gap and veer slightly right across the next field, now on an established unfenced track which continues to the left of a wood and across another field. It then skirts to the right of farm buildings to reach a T-junction with a tarmac drive, where you should turn right. At another T-junction, this time with **Forge Lane**, go right to follow this quiet lane for a quarter of a mile or so, back to the start.

Places of interest nearby

Groombridge Place, about 2 miles to the north, is a good place for a family outing. As well as the formal gardens, popular as a film setting, you can visit the 'Enchanted Forest' incorporating, amongst other features, a Mystic Pool and the Dinosaur and Dragon Valley. Live animals include deer, goats and a zeedonk, a cross between a zebra and a donkey. The gardens are open from mid-March to the end of October from 10 am to 5.30 pm. ☎ *01892 861444*.

The Blackboys Inn

The small village of Blackboys was once at the centre of the Wealden iron-smelting industry. The name means 'Black Wood' and may be derived from the soot which was a copious by-product of charcoal burning, carried out extensively in local woodlands to fuel the iron furnaces. The walk explores an intimate landscape of woods and fields to the north of the village, using segments of two long-distance footpaths across the Weald and which meet and diverge in the area, the Wealdway and the Vanguard Way.

THE PUB The **Blackboys Inn**, a tenanted house owned by Harveys Brewery of Lewes, is housed in a fine, old building dating from about 1200 and has been in business since 1389. The interior is divided into several small, cosy bar areas and a dining

Distance - 3½ miles.

OS Explorer 135 Ashdown Forest. GR 522204.

A gently undulating walk along field paths and quiet lanes.

Starting point The Blackboys Inn at Blackboys. Park in the pub car park with permission. Otherwise there should be room along School Lane which starts beside the pub.

How to get there Blackboys is set back on the north side of the B2192 Lewes-to-Heathfield road, about 4 miles west of Heathfield.

room and there is a large garden, bordered by a picturesque duck pond. The distinguished food menu, all home-cooked, features a high proportion of fish dishes, many with a generally Mediterranean flavour and character. A simpler bar menu is also on offer and includes ploughman's as well as some individual dishes. The beers are, as you might expect, all from Harveys and include, as well as the ubiquitous Sussex Bitter, a seasonal ale and the weaker Hadlow beer.

Opening times: 11 am to 11 pm on Monday to Saturday and 12 noon to 11 pm on Sunday. Food is served from 12 noon to 3 pm (4 pm on Sunday) and from 6 pm to 10 pm.
☎ 01825 890283

1 From the pub turn right beside the B2192. After about 200 yards turn right along the drive to a house called **Duckings**. About 50 yards short of a house, fork left up steps and along a permissive path. Shortly join and follow another drive, bordered by a series of flood lights, through to a lane and turn right.

2 After about 300 yards, just short of a cottage called **Pedlars**, turn right over a stile and follow a left field edge through to join the B2102. You are now following part of the **Wealdway**, a long-distance route for walkers linking **Eastbourne** with **Gravesend**. Turn right beside the road. After about 60 yards go left through a gate, follow an enclosed path to a stile and then head half right across a field to a second stile.

3 Follow the left edge of the next field to another stile from which a rather overgrown path follows power lines down through woodland to join a drive where you should turn left. At the bottom

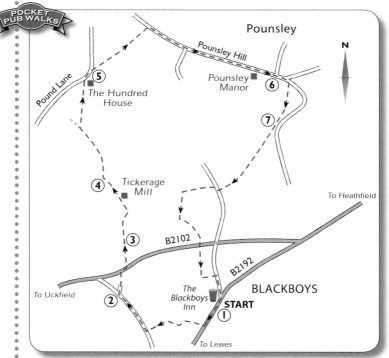

The attractive duck pond by the side of Blackboys Inn.

of the hill, pass to the left of a house and a pond at **Tickerage Mill** to reach a gate. Through the gate, the **Wealdway** goes off to the left but you should go ahead across a field, now briefly on part of another long-distance path, the **Vanguard Way**.

4 Go through a gate and continue uphill on a hedged path. Where the path comes out into the open, turn right across an arable field, where a path should be marked out through any growing crop. Go over a stile in a crossing hedge, maintain direction across the next field to join **Pound Lane** over another stile and turn right.

5 Soon after the lane rounds a left-hand bend, passing **The Hundred House** on the right, turn right on a narrow path which skirts to the left of a garden and continues along the left edge of two fields to join a lane, **Shepherds Hill** where you should turn right again. At a road junction, go ahead along **Pounsley Hill** which takes you down after a quarter of a mile to the tiny settlement of **Pounsley**.

⑥ Soon after passing **Pounsley Manor** on your right, go ahead along **Chapel Lane**, signposted to **Blackboys** and **Framfield,** ignoring two lanes off to the left. After another 100 yards or so, turn right along a narrow path, the start of which is squeezed between two gates. The first few yards may be overgrown, but things quickly improve. If impassable, the lane provides an alternative. A wooden causeway takes you over a boggy section. Continue to a stile and then climb diagonally across a field to reach **Chapel Lane** once more.

⑦ Don't join the lane. Instead, fork right along a rough access drive, signed as a bridleway which, beyond **Bridleway Cottage**, narrows to a path and takes you through to another lane. Turn right and, after a few yards, go left up steps, through a bridle gate and on between a fence and hedge. At a T-junction with a gravel track, turn left and, after 100 yards, go left opposite **Pheasant Cottage** along a signed path which climbs between high hedges and then allotments. At another junction go ahead out to the B2102. Cross the road and continue along **John Dann Close** opposite. A tarmac path skirts to the left of a recreation ground and then bears left out to join **School Lane**. Turn right for the short distance back to the start.

Places of interest nearby

Wilderness Wood at **Hadlow Down**, a few miles to the north along quiet lanes, is a 61-acre site which, although operated as commercial woodland, is also open to the public. A barn houses an exhibition and tea-room and there is a signed woodland trail, children's playground and gift shop. The owners organise a comprehensive programme of special events throughout the year. The wood is open daily from 10 am to 5.30 pm or dusk.

The Sussex Ox

From the tiny hamlet of Milton Street, tucked closely beneath the South Downs escarpment, the walk climbs steadily to reach a fine viewpoint on the summit of Wilmington Hill. It then traverses the ridge of Folkington Hill, using a path only recently opened up to the public. The return route follows part of an old coach road along the foot of the Downs to pass the village of Wilmington with good views of the spectacular chalk hill figure of the Long Man.

THE PUB Once a butcher's shop, the **Sussex Ox** is now a traditionally-furnished country pub, with brick and wooden floors in the bar areas, a dining room and, at the rear, a wooden-decked terrace and a two-acre garden, with fine views to the Downs.

Distance - 5½ miles.

OS Explorer 123 Eastbourne and Beachy Head. GR 534039.

A fairly strenuous walk, with one long steady climb to the top of the Downs.

Starting point The Sussex Ox at Milton Street. With permission, customers may park in the pub car park while on the walk.

How to get there Milton Street and the Sussex Ox are both signposted along a narrow lane which heads southwards from the A27 Lewes-to-Eastbourne road between Berwick and Polegate.

It is a free house serving Harveys Sussex Bitter and a choice of interesting guest beers such as Crouch Vale Brewers Gold. The menu is an extensive one, including unusual dishes such as rabbit burger and swordfish steak. The lunchtime snack menu includes filled baguettes and a three-cheese ploughman's. The Sussex Ox describes itself as a 'grown-up' pub but welcomes older children into the dining area.

Opening times: 11.30 am to 3 pm and 6 pm to 11 pm on Monday to Saturday and 12 noon to 3 pm and 6.30 pm to 10.30 pm on Sunday. Food is served daily from 12 noon to 2 pm and 6 pm to 9 pm.
☎ *01323 870840*

1 From the pub entrance, turn right and immediately right again, signposted to **Alfriston** and **Litlington**. After 200 yards, go left

over a stile and half right across a field where there should be a path trodden out through any growing crop. Go over a stile and bear right for a few yards to join a lane over a second stile.

2. Turn left, soon passing **Milton Court Farm** on your right. After about 300 yards, just short of a road junction, turn left along a track, signed as the **South Downs Way** which begins a steady climb on to the Downs.

3. Cross a lane and continue with the **South Downs Way** along a chalk and flint track between banks, passing to the left of a prominent covered reservoir and then curving to the right round the head of a grassy combe, **Ewe Dean**. Where the track divides, keep to the left-hand path which stays close to a fence as it crosses the shoulder of **Windover Hill**. The path passes above the head of the **Long Man of Wilmington** though the hill figure is barely recognisable from this angle.

4. A few yards after passing over a stile, bear half left, still climbing with a fence on your left. In the field corner, where the ground levels out, go through a gate and forward along the left edge of

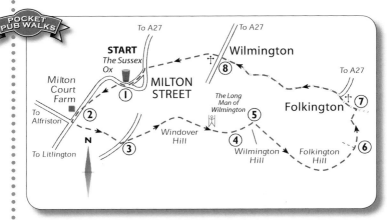

Firle Beacon seen from the path over Windover Hill.

a field, soon passing the trig point on the summit of **Wilmington Hill**. The all-round view from this point is superb.

5 Once through another gate, turn right along the ridge of **Folkington Hill**, with a fence on your right, walking on land made accessible under recent government legislation. After about two thirds of a mile, both path and fence curve to the left dropping down a grassy spur.

6 Go over a stile in a crossing fence and immediately veer half left across pasture, aiming for a waypost where you can bear

slightly left again, now on a trodden path. Cross a stile and drop obliquely down a steep grassy bank to a second stile. Now head out half right across a field where there is normally a trodden path. Join a wide grass path and bear right.

⑦ At a junction with a hard track, turn left. For the next mile or so you will be following part of the **Old Coach Road** along the foot of the **Downs**. At **Folkington**, where a road joins the track, turn left. A short there-and-back detour along the road from this point allows a visit to the isolated **Folkington church**, dating from the 13th century. Follow the track, through woods at first, then between high banks. Ignoring signed paths to the left and right, continue along the main track to reach the lane opposite **Wilmington church**.

⑧ Pass to the right of the church and to the left of an ancient yew tree, reputed to be 1,000 years old. At the far end of the churchyard, go through an iron gate, left for 5 yards along a drive, then right on an unfenced grassy strip. Follow this path through two fields, where you get an ideal view of the **Long Man of Wilmington**. About 100 yards short of the buildings at **Milton Street**, fork left along a narrower path to a stile and on to a second stile leading out to a lane. Turn left, then right at the fork and you are soon back at the pub.

Places of interest nearby

The village of **Alfriston**, a mile to the south of Milton Street along the Ouse valley, has much to offer. The 14th-century church stands on a mound overlooking the river and the village green, and is often called the 'Cathedral of the Downs', because of its solid construction. Nearby, the thatched, half-timbered **Alfriston Clergy House** was the first building to be acquired by the National Trust, back in 1896. ☎ 01323 870001 for details of opening times.

The Six Bells

This is a pleasant walk through a gently undulating landscape of fields, small woods and tiny streams in the Low Weald. The first half follows the well-established and signed Wealdway, but the return route is more challenging. Between points 5 and 6 you will need to follow the route description with particular care as the path is little-used and unsigned. The walk is probably at its best in the spring.

Distance - 4½ miles.

OS Explorer 123 Eastbourne and Beachy Head. GR 544143

A field path and woodland walk, without significant hills.

Starting point The Six Bells at Chiddingly. Park in the village car park a few yards from the pub along the access lane to Chiddingly church

How to get there Chiddingly is signposted northwards from the A22 Uckfield-to-Eastbourne road at Golden Cross, just east of the A22/B2124 junction, then left at Muddles Green.

THE PUB

The **Six Bells**, which has been serving ale since 1744, is an 'unimproved' village local in the best sense of the word, with low beamed ceilings and a brick floor in the central bar area and a separate dining area, both with open fires. The walls are adorned with old posters and there is a sheltered paved patio at the rear. It is a free house serving the local Harveys Sussex Bitter, Courage Directors and a regularly changing guest ale. The blackboard menu includes standard pub fare, as well as daily 'specials' such as cheesy leek and sweetcorn macaroni or chicken enchiladas with dips and salad.

Opening times: 11 am to 3 pm and 6 pm to 11 pm on Monday to Thursday, 11 am to midnight on Friday and Saturday and 12 noon to 10.30 pm on Sunday. Food is served from 12 noon to 2.30 pm and 6 pm to 10 pm on weekdays and all day on Friday, Saturday and Sunday.
☎ *01825 872227*

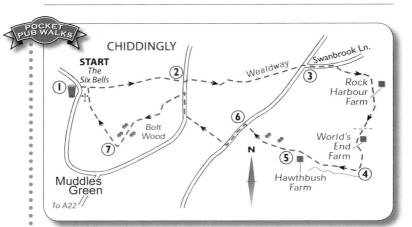

POCKET PUB WALKS

CHIDDINGLY

START
The Six Bells

Wealdway · Swanbrook Ln.

① ② ③

Rock Harbour Farm

Bolt Wood

⑥

World's End Farm

⑦ N ⑤ ④

Hawthbush Farm

Muddles Green

To A22

1️⃣ Start the walk along the access drive to **Chiddingly church**. Just past the church, fork left over a stile and head out across the middle of three fields, with stiles in intermediate crossing fences. For the first 2 miles you will be following part of the well-signed **Wealdway,** a long-distance route linking **Gravesend** and **Eastbourne**. A fenced path continues along an old earth dam at the head of a derelict pond to a footbridge, up through trees and across a field to join a lane where you should turn left.

2️⃣ After a few yards, go right through a gate, forward along a track and then along the left edge of two fields. At the bottom of the slope, go over a footbridge, cross a meadow to a stile and climb through a wood. Out of the wood, bear half left to join and follow the left edge of a large field. In the field corner, go left over a stile and head slightly right across a field to join a road in the far corner.

3️⃣ Bear left along the road and, after a few yards, fork right along **Swanbrook Lane**. After 250 yards, fork right along the drive to **Rock Harbour Farm**. After another 300 yards or so, follow this drive round to the right, past two farm entrances. The **Wealdway** shortly goes off to the left but you should continue ahead along the track. After about 200 yards, fork right through a gap in the hedge and head out across a field, diverging at about 45° from the hedge on your left. Go over a stile and plank bridge in a hedge and forward, skirting to the right of the buildings at **World's End Farm**.

4 About 40 yards short of a stream, turn right beside a fence on your right, walking parallel to the stream a little way away to your left. Go over a footbridge and ahead, with the stream still nearby on your left. In the field corner go over a stile and unbridged ditch and bear half right towards the buildings at **Hawthbush Farm**. Follow a track through the farmyard and along a right field edge. After about 100 yards, turn left along the top field edge, staying within the same field.

The Millennium Sculpture Garden at Chiddingly.

5 After 60 yards, go right through a wide gap in the hedge and head squarely out across a large field, where the path may be obscured by a growing crop. Aim to pass a few yards to the left of a group of large oak trees at the end of a promontory protruding towards you into the field. Go through a wide gap in the next hedge with the spire of **Chiddingly church** now directly ahead. Pass to the left of the end of another group of trees, this time protruding from the right and continue ahead across a field to join a road.

6 Turn left and, after about 250 yards, go right over a stile and follow the edge of two fields through to another road. Turn right and, after about 200 yards, go left along the rough drive to **Boltwood Stud**. After another 200 yards, go left over a stile and follow a well-trodden path between fences and then across pasture, passing to the left of an area of new tree planting. Cross an elaborate wooden causeway between two ponds and across a stream and continue through **Bolt Wood**, where you should ignore a left fork leading to a stile.

7 On the other side of the wood, turn right along an enclosed path. This path takes you back to **Chiddingly**, beside the wood, along a field edge, then through the recreation ground and the churchyard.

Places of interest nearby

About 5 miles south-east of Chiddingly is the moated **Michelham Priory**, founded in 1229 and occupied by the Augustinian Order until the dissolution. The priory with its Tudor wing is open to the public, together with a working forge and watermill. There is also a restaurant and picnic and play area. Opening times are from March to October, Tuesday to Sunday plus Bank Holiday Mondays and every Monday in August, 10.30 am to 5 pm. ☎ *01323 844224.*

10 **Old Heathfield**

The Star Inn

Some of the finest walking in Sussex can be found within the rich undulating countryside of the High Weald Area of Outstanding Natural Beauty, to the north of the county. It is a small-scale landscape which probably hasn't changed much since it was at the centre of the iron-smelting industry in the 16th and 17th centuries. The walk starts and finishes at the small hamlet of Old Heathfield, where the parish church and Star Inn stand well away from the large new settlement which grew up on the other side of Heathfield Park after the arrival of the railway.

THE PUB The date on the inn sign suggests that the **Star Inn** was built in 1348 and the story goes that it housed the stonemasons constructing the church next door. In all likelihood the pub was actually built about 200 years later, in the 15th century. The two modest bar and dining areas are full of character, with wood floors and low beams and outside there is a sheltered garden. It is a free house, offering, like so many Sussex pubs, the locally-brewed Harveys Sussex Bitter, as well as two more rotating guest beers. The high-quality menu favours a wide choice of seafood dishes.

Opening times: 11.30 am to 3.30 pm and 5.30 pm to 11 pm on Monday to Saturday and 12 noon to 3 pm and 7 pm to 10.30 pm on Sunday. Food is served from 12 noon to 3 pm and 7 pm to 9.30 pm (9 pm on Sunday).
☎ *01435 863570*

Distance - 3¾ miles.

OS Explorer 123 Eastbourne and Beachy Head. GR 599202.

A fairly hilly walk through woods and fields, and along an old trackway.

Starting point The Star Inn at Old Heathfield. Patrons may park in the car park with permission, or there is room beside the approach road to the village from the north, opposite the cricket ground.

How to get there *Old Heathfield is signposted from the B2096 Heathfield-to-Battle road about a mile east of Heathfield. The pub is tucked away on the south side of the parish church.*

Old Heathfield Walk 10

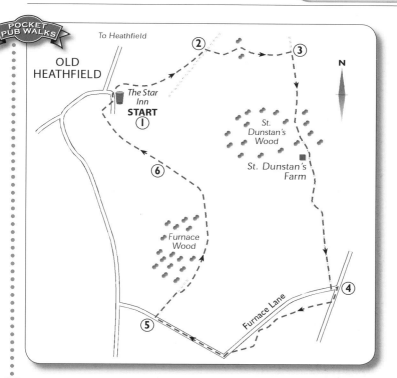

To Heathfield

OLD HEATHFIELD

The Star Inn
START
①

②

③

N

St. Dunstan's Wood

St. Dunstan's Farm

⑥

Furnace Wood

④

Furnace Lane

⑤

① From the pub car park, turn right to enter **Heathfield** churchyard. Pass to the right of the church and drop down along the right edge of the graveyard. Leave the church through an iron kissing-gate and bear very slightly left down across a field to find a stile and footbridge hidden in the trees in the bottom corner. Climb through scrub to a stile and continue in the same direction uphill across a field. Once over a stile beside a gate, turn left along a gravel track.

② After about 250 yards, turn right over a stile set back from the track and follow a path along a left field edge, with a good view

Old Heathfield.

southwards to the **Downs**. The path continues through a wood and along a left field edge to join a hedged grass track where you should turn right.

3 Follow this fine old track, probably an ancient highway, southwards. It passes through woodland and then along a left field edge before skirting well to the left of the buildings at **St Dunstan's Farm**, where it follows a right field boundary. An enclosed path continues, parallel to the drive from the farm, before joining and following the drive. At the bottom of the hill the official bridleway doglegs to the left to avoid a locked gate. Rejoin the drive and follow it out to join **Furnace Lane**.

4 Turn left, then immediately right at a road junction. After about 200 yards, turn right up overgrown steps to a stile and head out half left across two fields, with a stile between them. In the field corner, go over a stile and follow the right edge of the next field. Beyond a stile into the next field, veer half right across the corner of the field to rejoin **Furnace Lane** down steps cut in a bank. Turn left.

5 After about 300 yards, turn right along a wide access drive which, beyond a cottage, becomes an enclosed track for a while and then continues along a left field edge with **Furnace Wood** on the left. At the corner of the wood, veer half left through a gate and begin to drop downhill along an unfenced grass track, still with the wood nearby on your left.

6 From the bottom corner of the field, a track continues through a dip, with **Heathfield church** briefly in view ahead. A few yards beyond a bend to the left, turn right over a stile and follow a left field edge. In the field corner, cross a stile and continue beside a fence on the right. In the next field corner, go right through a gate and, after a few yards, left along a wide fenced path. Where this enclosed path ends, go ahead, joining and following iron railings on your right. After about 100 yards, go right through a kissing-gate, cross a drive and go half left across grass to join a lane. Turn left back to the pub, a few yards away.

Places of interest nearby

Bateman's, the fine 17th-century mansion near Burwash, a few miles to the east, was the home of Rudyard Kipling between 1902 and 1936. It is now owned and managed by the National Trust and many of the rooms are furnished much as they were when Kipling lived there. The house and garden are open from mid-March to October except on Thursdays and Fridays. ☎ *01435 882302.*

11 Cowbeech

The Merrie Harriers

The village of Cowbeech lies a few miles to the north
of Hailsham, in a relatively remote area on the southern
slopes of the High Weald. Some of the paths in the parish
are little-used and tend to become overgrown but you will be
pleased to know that you should have no problems at all on
this pleasant circuit. It is along established and well-signed paths
traversing a patchwork of woods and fields to the south of the
village and rising to Cowbeech Hill, where there are good views
southwards towards the distant line of the South Downs.

THE PUB Once a coaching Inn, the **Merrie Harriers** is now a friendly
village local, housed in a white, weather-boarded building
dating back to 1624. The beamed bar area has a large
inglenook fireplace and there is a spacious dining area at the

Distance - 4½ miles.

OS Explorer 123 Eastbourne and Beachy Head. GR 619146.

An easy, gently undulating walk through woodland and along field paths.

Starting point The Merrie Harriers pub at Cowbeech. The car park can be used by pub customers while on the walk but please ask permission first. Alternatively there is room to park along the village street.

How to get there Cowbeech is signposted from the A271 Hailsham-to-Herstmonceux road at Magham Down about 2 miles from Hailsham and the pub is on the main street through the village.

rear, converted from a conservatory and overlooking the garden. It is a free house offering Harveys Sussex Bitter and a regularly changing guest beer. As well as a substantial and varied restaurant menu, there is a separate bar menu which includes sandwiches with some interesting fillings, such as crayfish with lemon mayonnaise or mature cheddar with pear chutney. Children are allowed in the dining area and dogs are permitted in the bar.

Opening times: 11.30 am to 3 pm and 6 pm to 11 pm on weekdays and 12 noon to 4 pm and 6 pm to 10.30 pm on Sunday. Food is served from 12 noon to 2 pm daily.
☎ *01323 833108*

1 From the pub turn right and head southwards. A few yards past the speed de-restriction signs at the edge of the village, turn right

along a track to a gate, set back from the road. Climb a bank and follow a right field edge. From the field corner continue along a waymarked route through a wood, ignoring all other paths.

2 Leave the wood over a stile and head half left across a field to a gate into another wood. Immediately inside this wood, fork left and, shortly, where the path divides again, keep right. Leave the wood through a gate and veer slightly left across a field to another gate and steps which go down to join a lane on a bend. Bear right along the lane (in effect, almost straight on).

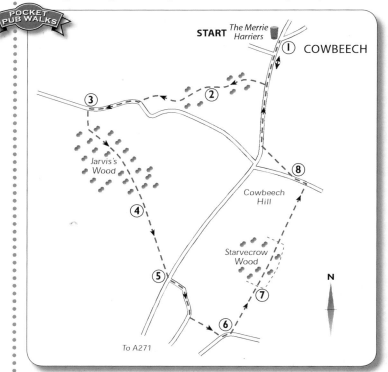

The route through Jarvis's Wood.

3 After about 350 yards, turn left through a gate, walk beneath a metal height barrier and go forward along a track. After 70 yards, fork left to enter **Jarvis's Wood**. After skirting to the left of a pond, fork right and, a little further on, fork left, following waymarks. The path narrows, dropping to a stream crossing before climbing steeply.

4 Leave the wood and go ahead along a left field edge, with a distant view of the **South Downs**. From the field corner, maintain direction now with the remains of a fence line on your right. In a dip, where you have a choice of two gates ahead, go through the one on the left and climb, passing between a bungalow and garden on your left and farm buildings on your right, to join a road.

5 Cross the road and follow the lane opposite. After about 400 yards, turn left over a stile and follow a path within a wooded strip and then beside a high garden fence to join a road and turn left.

[6] After a few yards, go left into the start of a track and immediately go left again through a gate. Now head out across the middle of a field, diverging at about 30 degrees from the hedge on your right and aiming for a gate in the far left corner (not the bridlegate over to your left which is for toll riders only). Maintain direction up across the next field to enter **Starvecrow Wood** over a stile half hidden behind a tree.

[7] Continue with the main path through the wood, ignoring all side paths. Leave the wood over a stile and continue on a straight course along the right edge of two fields, rising steadily. Where the path levels out, pause to look back across the **Weald** to a long segment of the **South Downs** escarpment in distant view. At the end of the second field, the path feeds into an access drive which you can follow out to the road at **Cowbeech Hill**. Turn left. ▸

[8] Just past a house called **The Acorns** on the right, fork right along a tarmac drive. After 70 yards, fork right through a swing gate and follow a waymarked path across four small enclosures punctuated by gates and stiles. Join a road and follow it to the right for half a mile back into **Cowbeech.**

Places of interest nearby

Pevensey Castle, about 6 miles to the south of **Cowbeech** across **Pevensey Levels**, is a place of great historic interest. It comprises the remains of a Norman castle built within a Roman fort at the mouth of a river, where William the Conqueror landed in 1066. Held and subsequently besieged many times over the centuries, the ruins are now preserved and are open to the public daily from April to October and at weekends during the winter months. ☎ *01323 460382.*

12 **Boreham Street**

The Bulls Head

This walk explores the gentle southern slopes of the High Weald where the ground begins to level out towards the wide-open, restored marshland of the Pevensey Levels. It follows generally well-maintained paths and tracks through woods and fields, partly along the 1066 Country Walk, a long-distance route linking Eastbourne and Rye. The 4½-mile walk option passes close to Herstmonceux Castle and offers good views of the castle as well as the domes of the former Royal Greenwich Observatory nearby.

Distance - 2½ miles or 4½ miles.

OS Explorer 124 Hasting and Bexhill. GR 666113.

An easy, fairly level walk. May be muddy in places after rain.

Starting point The Bull's Head at Boreham Street. You may park in the pub car park with prior permission if also patronising the pub.

How to get there Boreham Street is on the A271 between Hailsham and Bexhill.

THE PUB

The 17th-century **Bull's Head** was the first pub in Sussex to be owned and run on a tenancy by Harvey's Brewery of Lewes. It has recently undergone extensive refurbishment, though without the loss of its village pub character. The bar opens into a cosy and secluded dining area and there is a garden and children's play area at the rear. The beers, as might be expected, come from Harveys – their Sussex Bitter supplemented by an appropriate seasonal ale. The large menu offers several seafood dishes, including mussels prepared as marinieres, Provençale or à la crème. Lunchtime snacks include filled baguettes and jacket potatoes. Children are allowed in the dining area, as are dogs in the bar.

Opening times: 12 noon to 3 pm and 6 pm to 11 pm on weekdays and 12 noon to about 4 pm on Sundays. The pub is closed on Sunday evenings. Food is served from 12 noon to 2 pm (2.30 pm on Sunday) and from 6 pm to 8.30 pm (except on Sunday). ☎ 01323 831981

[1] From the pub, turn left beside the road**.** After about 150 yards, turn left again along an enclosed path, signed as the **1066 Country Walk** which you will be following for the next 2 miles. Where the enclosed path ends, keep to the left edge of the first field and the right edge of a second field. Beyond a stile in the next field corner, veer slightly left across undulating pasture to another stile. Now follow a well-signed and stiled route across several paddocks to join a lane and turn right.

[2] After a few yards, go through the second gate on the left and keep to the right edge of a large field. After about a quarter of a mile, at the field corner, fork right into woodland and follow the top of a raised bank through the trees to a stile. Continue along a left field edge out to a road and turn right.

[3] After 200 yards, just short of the entrance to **Herstmonceux Castle and Science Centre**, turn left along a path signed as a

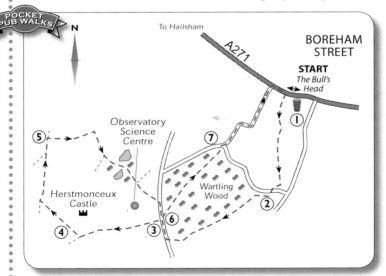

Herstmonceux Castle.

bridleway to **Herstmonceux church**. *(For the shorter walk turn right here)*. To the right, across the fields, you get a good view of the domes of the former **Royal Greenwich Observatory**. After almost half a mile, the path comes out into the open. After a few more yards, at a waymarker next to a stunted sweet chestnut tree, turn right across grass, parting company with the 1066 walk. From this path you get an excellent view of **Herstmonceux Castle**. The fine, moated castle was one of the first large brick-built structures in the country and now probably the oldest brick building still standing. It dates from the 15th century but by 1911 had fallen into ruins and was extensively renovated. For 40 years, following the Second World War, it housed the Royal Greenwich Observatory.

4 Go over a stile to enter a short enclosed path, cross the drive to the castle and the stile opposite and cross a field to enter woodland. A few yards inside the wood, fork left and, after

60 yards, at a T-junction with a more substantial path, turn right, then ignore an immediate left fork. Leave the wood through a bridlegate and veer slightly right, dropping downhill and aiming for a solitary tree.

5 A few yards past this tree, turn right through a bridlegate and follow a faint unfenced grassy path along a valley. Go through a second bridlegate, right through a third gate and ahead on a narrow path through scrub which widens as it enters woodland. Soon after crossing an earth dam with a reed-filled pond on the left, fork right along a narrower path with a fence on your right. Where the path opens out, go ahead across a field to join a road in the far left field corner. Turn right.

6 After a few yards you will find yourself back at point 3 where you should turn left over a stile into **Wartling Wood** and go ahead along a woodland path. At a T-junction with a wider path, turn left. Go straight across an eroded crossing track, continuing along a narrower path through the wood which brings you out to a lane.

7 Turn left and, immediately, at a road junction, go right along **Wood Lane.** Follow the lane for about a quarter of a mile out to the A271 and turn right back into **Boreham Street.**

Places of interest nearby

The Observatory Science Centre, a short distance from point 3 on the walk, was built to contain the telescopes of the Royal Greenwich Observatory but now houses a large collection of science-related 'hands-on' exhibits and makes a great family day out. It is open daily from the end of January to November. ☎ *01323 832731.*

The gardens of nearby **Herstmonceux Castle** (though not the castle itself) are also open to the public. ☎ *01323 833816*

The Plough

Although only two miles, as the crow flies, from the built-up area of Hastings, the village of Crowhurst is a peaceful backwater, tucked down in a valley. The church, although largely rebuilt in 1856, retains a 15th-century tower. Carved on the tower door is the Pelham Buckle, the insignia of a well-known local family, which is a feature of several Sussex churches, including the one at Chiddingly (see Walk 9). This relaxing walk takes us through a landscape of woods and fields.

THE PUB The **Plough** has been in business since 1835 but was extensively restored after being hit by a bomb in 1943. Occupying a secluded position at the foot of a wooded slope, it offers a warm welcome to walkers in its large open-plan bar or the dining extension at the rear. It is a freehouse serving beer from two local breweries, Harveys of Lewes and Whites of Pebsham. The good traditional pub menu is mostly homemade and includes such favourites as cottage pie and macaroni cheese. There is also a separate lunchtime snack menu, embracing a choice of ploughman's, sandwiches and filled baguettes.

Opening times: 11.30 am to 2.30 pm on Monday to Friday, 11.30 am to 11 pm on Saturday and 12 noon to 4 pm and 6 pm to 10.30 pm on Sunday. Food is served every lunchtime and on Thursday, Friday and Saturday evenings.
☎ *01424 830310*

1 From the pub, turn right along the road, soon joining the **1066 Bexhill Link Walk** which comes in from the right and which you will be following for the first half mile of the walk. After

Distance - 3½ miles.

OS Explorer 124 Hastings and Bexhill. GR 759117.

A gently undulating walk, mostly along good paths, tracks and a quiet country lane. One short section can get overgrown and boggy.

Starting point The Plough at Crowhurst. Patrons may park in the pub car park with permission while on the walk. Otherwise park along Station Road, starting the walk at point 2.

How to get there *Crowhurst is signposted from the B2092 ring road to the west of Hastings or can be reached from the A2100 between Battle and Hastings.*

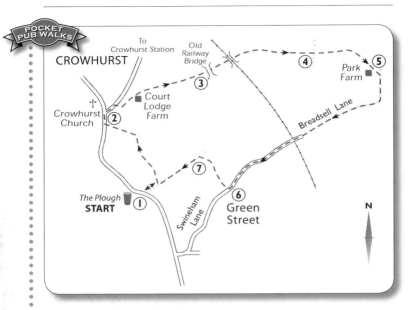

POCKET
PUB WALKS

To
Crowhurst Station

CROWHURST

Old
Railway
Bridge

④

Park
Farm

⑤

③

Court
Lodge
Farm

Crowhurst
Church ②

Breadsell Lane

⑦

The Plough
START ①

Swineham
Lane

⑥
Green
Street

N

200 yards, turn left along **Sampsons Lane**, and after a little over 100 yards, go left over a stile and forward along a left field edge with a tiny stream on your left. After about 350 yards, go left over a footbridge, forward along a right field to join a lane and turn right.

[2] Shortly, when almost opposite **Crowhurst church** on the left, turn right along **Station Road**. The church, although heavily restored, has a 15th-century tower. Nearby are the fragmented remains of a 13th-century manor house. After a few yards along **Station Road**, fork right along the concrete drive to **Court Lodge Farm** which bends round to the left and passes beneath the central section of an open-sided barn, continuing as a gravelled track, fenced on the left. After passing between two ponds, go ahead on a faint path which climbs across the middle of a large area of pasture.

3 Pass under an impressive brick bridge which once carried a branch of the railway to **Bexhill** and then pass through an altogether more utilitarian metal-lined tubular tunnel beneath the still-functioning railway line to **Hastings.** A path continues through woodland and then uphill along a left field edge with a wood on your left before becoming a more substantial track.

4 Go straight over a crossing track and ahead, still on a hard-based track. From this point you are high enough to get a distant view southwards and westwards to the hills above **Eastbourne** and a glimpse of the sea between **Bexhill** and **Hastings**. At the bottom of the hill, a few yards after passing over a culvert, fork right

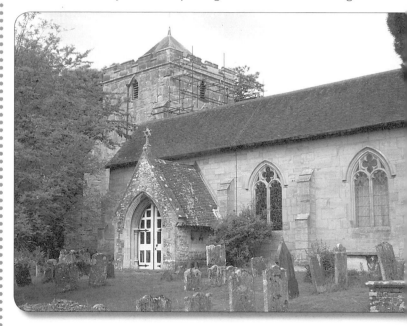

Crowhurst church

along a grassy path, climbing beside a fence to rejoin the track which has come round a hair-pin bend to meet you. Turn right.

5 Pass through the complex of buildings at **Park Farm** to reach a T-junction with a metalled drive where you should turn right. Follow this drive, marked as **Breadsell Lane** on the Explorer Map. After a little over a quarter of a mile, it crosses the railway and becomes a public road, **Swineham Lane**, which after another quarter of a mile or so, brings you to the tiny settlement of **Green Street**.

6 A few yards after passing a charming, tile-hung, converted oast house on the right, look out for the far from obvious start of a path into woodland on your right. It is to be found to the left of a gate and is marked by a stone plinth. This path, always evident underfoot but overgrown with brambles and nettles in the summer, winds through the wood and then drops down between banks, wider but boggy underfoot in places. Shortly go left over a stile and follow another short, potentially overgrown, path which takes you out to join the drive from a cottage.

7 Turn left and follow this drive down into the valley, finally reversing your outgoing route along **Sampsons Lane** and then right along the road for 200 yards or so back to the pub.

Places of interest nearby

The town of **Battle** is within easy reach, about 4 miles to the north. Famous for the **Battle of Hastings**, it is also the site of **Battle Abbey**, built by William the Conqueror to commemorate the battle. Parts of the abbey and the battlefield are open daily throughout the year from 10 am to 6 pm (4 pm in winter). *For more information* ☎ *01424 773792*.

14 Sedlescombe

The Queen's Head

Sedlescombe, frequent winner of best-kept village awards, is a delightful place to start a walk. The long village street, flanked by a green, is lined by a number of attractive period houses, its original prosperity arising from the fact that the village was, during the 16th and 17th centuries, at the centre of the iron-smelting industry. The walk explores an intimate landscape of small woods and fields to the north and east of Sedlescombe.

THE PUB The **Queen's Head** dates from the 14th century and was once a coaching inn on the road to Hastings. It enjoys a beautiful setting, facing on to the village green. The spacious bar area is complemented by a new restaurant, converted from a former pool room. It is now part of the Enterprise Inn chain but has retained its individuality as a welcoming country pub.

The main menu of popular pub favourites is supplemented by a choice of snacks at lunchtime, including 'triple-layer' sandwiches or filled baguettes. Harveys Sussex Bitter is always available on hand pump, supplemented by a rotating guest beer. Children and dogs are welcome.

Opening times: 11 am to 3 pm and 6 pm to 11.30 pm on Monday to Friday, 11 am to 12 midnight on Saturday and 12 noon to 11 pm on Sunday. Food is served daily from 12 noon to 2.30 pm and 7 pm to 9.30 pm except Monday evening.
☎ *01424 870228*

1 From the entrance to the village car park, turn left into **Gammons Way** and immediately, at a road junction, turn right. After less than 100 yards, just short of a 30 mph road sign, turn left along a narrow tarmac twitten (passageway). Where this ends, join and go ahead along an estate road.

Distance - 3 miles.

OS Explorer 124 Hastings and Bexhill. GR 782180.

An undulating walk with several ups and downs, using field and woodland paths and one section along a quiet country lane.

Starting point Sedlescombe village car park, within a few yards of the Queen's Head pub.

How to get there *Sedlescombe is on the B2244 road which is signposted from the A21 about 6 miles north of Hastings. The village car park is signed to the east of the village street, tucked away behind the pub.*

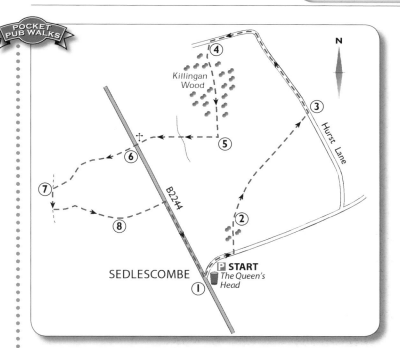

N

Killingan Wood

Hurst Lane

B2244

SEDLESCOMBE

START
The Queen's Head

① ② ③ ④ ⑤ ⑥ ⑦ ⑧

[2] At the end of this road, go forward over a stile beside a gate and ahead beside a left-hand fence to reach another stile. The arrow on the stile indicates the direction across a field of rough pasture but if this is badly overgrown you may find it easier to follow the left field edge round, where there is a faint path. Either way, from the lowest point on the other side of the field a signed and stiled path continues through a wood, crossing a stream. Climb across the next field where the line of the path is marked by a solitary oak tree, to join **Hurst Lane** over a stile.

[3] Turn left and, after about a quarter of a mile, follow the lane round to the left. After another 300 yards, on reaching a small parking area on the left, turn left along a wide path into **Killingan Wood**.

Looking towards Sedlescombe church from point 5 of the walk.

[4] A few yards inside the wood, turn left over a sleeper bridge and follow a well-trodden path as it winds in a generally southerly direction through this beautiful area of woodland. Just short of a junction with an unmade drive, go right through a metal kissing-gate into a field corner and drop gently downhill along the left edge of two fields, with a fine view ahead across the valley of the **River Line**. Also in sight to the right is **Sedlescombe church**, your next objective.

[5] About 50 yards into the second field, turn squarely right and head for the church, now almost hidden by trees. Drop down across a large meadow. At the bottom of the hill, go over a new footbridge and climb within an enclosed path which takes you out via a house drive to join a road. The church is now a few yards to the right and is worth the short detour.

6 Cross the road and follow the drive to **Beech House** opposite. Walk along the right edge of a lawn to find a gate from which an enclosed path continues. Where this path ends, go ahead, dropping down into the next valley along the right edge of two hay meadows. Cross a wide concrete bridge, go half left to a stile and climb along the left edge of a vineyard.

7 In the field corner, go over a stile and left along a wide grassy track. After 100 yards you have a choice of two gates ahead. Go through the one on the left and turn left for 10 yards to a stile from which a narrow fenced path drops down into the valley. Over another stile, continue beside a left-hand fence, passing to the right of a pond, not marked on OS maps.

8 Go over another stile, cross a stream within a belt of woodland to reach a gate and then veer slightly right up across a meadow to a stile, soon in sight. Maintain direction across a field to a gate and, leaving a small copse on your left, head out across another field, diverging at about 20 degrees from the right field boundary. Go over a stile to the left of a house and skirt to the left of this house and its garden to join a road. Turn right back into **Sedlescombe**.

Places of interest nearby

Bodiam Castle, about 5 miles to the north, is a perfect embodiment of a fairytale moated castle. Built in the 14th century, it was dismantled during the Civil War after a siege. Acquired by Lord Curzon in 1917, it has been carefully restored as a romantic ruin, which appears impressively intact from the outside. It is now owned by the National Trust and open daily from February to October and at weekends during the other winter months. ☎ 01580 830212

15 Icklesham

The Queen's Head

From the pub, splendidly situated on a ridge overlooking the wide valley of the River Brede, the walk sets out along the well established and clearly signed 1066 Country Walk, descending briefly towards the Brede valley before climbing back over the ridge. The return route along less-well-used paths requires some care with navigation as it is largely unsigned. It takes in the northern slopes of the more intimate valley of the Pannel Stream, diverting to visit Icklesham church, first established in AD 722 and containing well-preserved features from the 11th and 12th centuries.

THE PUB The **Queen's Head** is housed in a picturesque tile-hung building, dating from 1632 and first established as an ale house in 1831. The cosy and characterful interior is on three levels and is notable for a wealth of oak beams, as well as a

Distance - 3 ¾ miles.

OS Explorer 124 Hastings and Bexhill or 125 Romney Marsh. GR 878167.

A gently undulating walk along field paths and tracks.

Starting point The Queen's Head in Icklesham. Park in the pub car park with permission or in the village recreation ground car park.

How to get there The Queen's Head is signposted northwards from the A259 Hastings-to-Rye road along Parsonage Lane. The recreation ground car park is on the south side of the A259, a few yards west of the A259/Parsonage Lane junction.

fine old inglenook fireplace. The garden offers a delightful view along the Brede valley towards the hill-top town of Rye. It is a free house offering a wide and regularly rotated choice of well-kept beers. The extensive menu embraces a choice of homemade pies and a good vegetarian selection, as well as the usual range of bar snacks.

Opening times: 11 am to 11 pm on Monday to Saturday and 12 noon to 10.30 pm on Sunday. Food is served from 12 noon to 2.45 pm and 6.15 pm to 9.45 pm on Monday to Friday and from 12 noon to 9.45 pm on Sunday.
☎ *01424 814552*

[1] From the pub, set out along **Parsonage Lane**, walking away from the A259 and signed with a red logo as part of the **1066 Country Walk**, a long-distance route linking the town of **Rye** with the historic sites of **Battle Abbey** and **Pevensey Castle**.

The lane becomes, in turn, a rough track and then a hedged path.

[2] Shortly go right over a stile and drop downhill along a right field edge. A faintly trodden path with fine views across the valley of the **River Brede** continues more steeply down a slope to a stile. Over the stile go forward walking parallel to the meandering left field edge. Cross a stile in the corner and go ahead along the right edge of two fields and then a drive which climbs out of the valley.

[3] Follow a track as it skirts to the right of the buildings at **Brook Farm**. Rejoin the track which has come straight through the buildings and follow it out to a lane. The **1066 Country Walk**

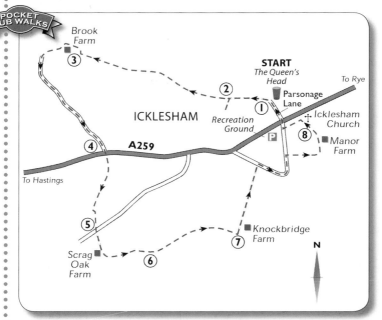

Approaching Brook Farm.

soon goes off to the right but you should carry on along the lane
following it for almost half a mile out to the A259.

4️⃣ Cross the main road, go over the stile opposite and head out
across a field towards a gate. Pass to the right of the gate (i.e.
not through it), continuing beside a left-hand fence. A trodden
path curves to the right and, after 30 yards, you turn left along a
woodland path. Cross a drive and go ahead with a close-boarded
fence on your left. Descend to a footbridge and stile and bear left
along the left edge of a young tree plantation. In the field corner
go left through a gate and, after five yards, right along a narrow
path between fence and hedge out to a lane.

5️⃣ Turn left and, after a few yards, go right along the drive to
Scrag Oak Farm. In the farmyard, turn left, passing to the left
of buildings and continuing along a left field edge. Over to your
right is the valley of the **Pannel Stream**, a minor tributary of the
Brede, with the spire of **Pett church** in view on the skyline.

6 In the field corner go through a wide gap and bear right along a right field edge. After about 200 yards, side-step to the right over the second of two stiles and resume your previous direction, now dropping gently down with a fence and hedge on your left. At the bottom of the hill go through a gate and climb with a hedge now on your right. In the top field corner go through a gate and keep close to the left edge of the next field, skirting to the right of a garden.

7 After about 100 yards, turn left through the farmyard at **Knockbridge Farm** and go ahead along the access drive from the farm out to a lane. Turn right. At a road junction go left and, after a few yards, turn right along the access drive to a pair of garages. Go over a stile beside a gate and shortly right and left to follow the right edge of an orchard. Join a drive and turn left passing to the left of the nicely converted twin oast house at **Manor Farm**.

8 Shortly fork left along a grassy path and soon look out for a path on the right providing access to **Icklesham church**, a building of great architectural interest, dating from the 12th century, with a Norman tower. Follow the access path from the church out to **Workhouse Lane**. Turn right, cross the A259 and follow **Parsonage Lane** back to the pub.

Places of interest nearby

The ancient hilltop towns of **Winchelsea** and **Rye**, two of the original Cinque Ports, are both within easy reach of Icklesham, eastwards along the A259. Rye is notable for its cobbled streets and ancient buildings and Winchelsea has streets laid out on a chequer-board pattern by Edward I in 1292. Although subsequently ravaged by French raiders, three of its ancient gatehouses and the 14th-century church survive.